New Orleans
New Elegance

New Orleans
New Elegance

Kerri McCaffety

Introduction by Julia Reed

THE MONACELLI PRESS

Copyright © 2012 The Monacelli Press
Photographs copyright © 2012 Kerri McCaffety
Introduction copyright © 2012 Julia Reed
All rights reserved.

Published in the United States by The Monacelli Press

Library of Congress Control Number: 2012932702

ISBN 978-158093-332-2

10 9 8 7 6 5 4 3 2 1

First edition

Design: Susan Evans, *Design per se,* New York

Printed in China

www.monacellipress.com

	Introduction – Julia Reed	6
I.	The Creole Legacy	12
II.	Eclectic to Eccentric	34
III.	Fresh Creole	50
IV.	New New Orleans Style	128
	Resources	216
	Acknowledgments	219

Contents

Toward the end of Lyle Saxon's 1928 book *Fabulous New Orleans,* there's a chapter called "The New New Orleans." In it, the author bemoans the arrival of office buildings and chain stores; he worries that the city has "spread" so much that visitors might leave without ever having set foot in the Vieux Carré. Mostly though, he mourns the Sazerac cocktail and absinthe frappe "of sainted memory," the Ramos gin fizz once "prepared almost as a religious ceremony." Saxon was writing in the midst of Prohibition; he believed that the city's "alcoholic beverages of unsurpassed excellence" would remain relics of the past. "Perhaps it is for the greater good," he wrote, a tad unconvincingly, "but New Orleans misses the stimulation."

In the New Orleans of today, Saxon would find a further expanded city and a lot more office buildings, but, happily, stimulation would not be a problem. Alcohol is available twenty-four hours a day, seven days a week in restaurants, bars, grocery stores, and drugstores; even the 1912 ban on absinthe has been lifted. More important, America's recent cocktail renaissance has, not surprisingly, reached its apotheosis in the city where the first-ever cocktail (a precursor of Saxon's "sainted" Sazerac) is said to have been mixed.

Across the city, countless fizzes and frappes are crafted with the old ceremonial devotion in sleek new bars decorated with everything from midcentury modern fixtures and furniture to white Ultrasuede banquettes. Fittingly, what's happening in the bar scene works as a metaphor for the new New Orleans itself, particularly in terms of style. While there's an acknowledgment, and in some cases a revival, of those things that made the city's past so special, there's a far less encumbered approach toward how that past is integrated into the way we live today. While Saxon would still recognize the "high white columns" of Garden District houses and the "overhanging balconies" of his beloved French Quarter, he would be astonished by some of the interiors that lie behind them.

New New Orleans Style

The ironic thing is that for the first two hundred years of New Orleans's existence, the city's style was always new. Beginning with the first wooden hut built in 1718 by French-Canadian explorer Jean Baptiste, Sieur de Bienville, who founded the city for the French, the look of the place was reinvented and augmented with each new building advance (the availability of bricks, the introduction of cast-iron decoration) and each new wave of settlers of hugely varying nationalities and class. It was a pattern that continued until just before Saxon wrote his book. Like the music and cuisine that also defines New Orleans, the city's architecture and the way its inhabitants did up their interiors was historically rooted in an intricate cross-pollinization of cultures and influences, ranging from the earliest French, Spanish, African, English, and Caribbean to the German, Irish, Italian, and Latin American that came later.

First, there are the extraordinarily varied house forms themselves. In the late eighteenth century, colonial planters erected West Indies–inspired raised houses featuring multiple sets of French doors and galleries suitable to the climate. After 1800, French Quarter merchants built the more urban four-room Creole cottages and two- and three-story townhouses. With the arrival of English-speaking Americans, townhouses were built with hallways and rooms designated for specific uses. The working classes who arrived in the 1840s needed simple, affordable housing and the solution was whole neighborhoods comprised of "shotguns" (so named because if a shotgun was fired through the front door, its pellets could fly through the straight succession of rooms and exit out the back without hitting a thing).

The period between 1830 and 1862 was the most prosperous—and flamboyant—in New Orleans history. The city became America's wealthiest city as well as its fourth largest. The ambitious English and American businessmen shut out of the French Quarter by the aristocratic Creoles (loosely, all those descended from the colonial settlers, especially the French and Spanish) were eager to show off their newly acquired fortunes with freestanding Greek revival double-galleried houses and raised cottages and fancy Italianate villas in the Garden District, where they ultimately settled. After the Civil War, both the facades and interiors of these grand manses became even more ornate. Such ordinarily restrained Greek revival motifs as dentils, Greek key surrounds, and Doric columns morphed into more florid examples. Queen Anne houses featured porches and towers and as many as five colors on a single exterior. Carved marble mantels and plaster ceiling medallions began to look as though they contained virtual flower arrangements or fruit baskets.

By this time the footprint of the city had become a bit of a fruit basket as well. In the Francophone downtown, two neighborhoods bordering the Quarter had been established: Treme, settled in the eighteenth and nineteenth centuries by free people of color and freed slaves, and the Faubourgs Marigny and Bywater, back-to-back areas that had arisen largely from the plantation of Bernard de Marigny, which was subdivided in the early nineteenth century.

The rest of the city expanded uptown in a rough line that followed the Mississippi. First came the creation of the "American District," a narrow strip between the Quarter and the Livaudais Plantation. Composed of attached rowhouses (primarily built from townhouse plans imported from London and the American northeast) and the warehouses needed to accommodate the increasingly busy port, the area is now referred to as the Warehouse District (though in the last decade or so, most of the warehouses have been converted into chic apartments or condos). Next, in the early 1830s, the Livaudais Plantation was subdivided into spacious Garden District lots, and not long afterward, working-class Irish, German, and Italian settlers moved into a long strip running alongside the river (near the docks) and adjacent to the Garden District that is still known as the Irish Channel. For the rest of the nineteenth century, expansion continued on up to the parish line in a jumble of neighborhoods collectively referred to as Uptown, which also encompasses Audubon Park.

In the early twentieth century, New Orleans, like the rest of the country, saw the rise of the bungalow style and revivals of Georgian and Spanish Colonial and Tudor architecture, but the almost breakneck evolution of the city's architecture slowed considerably. As early as the 1920s, when Saxon was in residence, New Orleans itself had already acquired a slightly worn affect. Writers like Saxon, Sherwood Anderson, William Faulkner, Tennessee Williams, and others were drawn to the city's faded elegance and sense of decay, and were among the first to promulgate the notion of New Orleans as a romantic refuge from the modern world. Williams, who called New Orleans his "spiritual home," wrote memorably of time standing still—and, increasingly, it did, but not always in the most charming of ways.

During the last half of the twentieth century, the city expanded well past the path of the river into such "suburbs" as Lakeview, but there was little other positive growth. New Orleans was marked by a stagnant economy, failing public schools, a huge spike in the crime rate, and civic apathy in the face of an appallingly corrupt government. The overall mood translated into a certain "style apathy" as well. The city had long been a place where families passed portraits, furniture (often with same increasingly threadbare upholstery), and even houses down through generations.

Two blocks away from my own house sits the oldest house in the Garden District, a raised "cottage" where the descendants of the family who bought it just after the Civil War still live. A block in the other direction is the house where Jefferson Davis breathed his last, complete with plaque commemorating the event and heavy curtains hanging from ornate cornices visible from the street.

To a large swath of the populace, the past had become something of a pastime (and indeed, where tourists were concerned, an industry). Parlors contained glass cases of Mardi Gras memorabilia, which sometimes included actual dress forms featuring somebody's grandmother's Queen of Comus gown. Even in freshly decorated houses, the emphasis was on all things French, as though the city was not the international melting pot that had always set it apart. Walker Percy called New Orleans America's "most European city," but for a great many locals—and their decorators—Europe was limited to the France of Louis Philippe.

And it wasn't just the natives that got caught up in the allure of all things French and old, if not literally moldering. For one of my first apartments in the Quarter, I bought a French chair with tattered needlepoint upholstery and another with no seat at all. At that point, I lived on the third floor of a mostly untouched early-nineteenth-century porte-cochere townhouse, whose floors were so rotted that my high heels poked holes in them. In that environment, my purchases somehow looked entirely normal, as did the foxed and water-stained bird prints and threadbare rugs I plundered from my mother's attic reject pile. Context was all and the context was crumbling.

To be fair, there were notable exceptions. As early as the 1980s, designers Gerrie Bremermann, Ann Dupuy and Ann Holden, and John Chrestia were among those who became nationally well known for their more modern sensibilities. They knew how to mix old with new; they lightened up everything from color palettes to curtain treatments. But they made a name for themselves precisely because they were not the norm. Then, of course, in 2005, the word "norm" abruptly ceased to have any meaning. There is nothing like a hurricane followed by an epic flood to upset the order of things and blow in some literal winds of change.

New Orleans post-Katrina is a city with a far more diverse—and growing—economy, a school system with a chance, and a responsible city government coupled with vigorous civic involvement. The populace was forced to realize that you do get the city you deserve, and today's New Orleans is a markedly different—and forward looking—place.

Given the city's current atmosphere, living in a shrine to the past no longer feels appropriate. There is also the fact that hundreds of thousands of houses were either destroyed or damaged, and countless personal items lost. A lot of people had no choice but to start over. In style terms, this has translated into a look that can best be described as liberated. Keeping Great Aunt Jane's settee covered with the same faded silk brocade she herself inherited with it no longer seems of paramount importance in a city where so many lost so much, including the equivalent of Great Aunt Jane.

Again, a useful comparison can be found in the world of bars and restaurants. Post-Katrina, more and more New Orleans chefs began putting their own stamps on cooking based in Creole and Cajun traditions, and designers and homeowners began deconstructing and tweaking traditions of their own. Just as the food became cleaner, lighter, possessed of global influences, so too did interiors. In neither case, food or décor, was the baby thrown out with the bathwater—local ingredients and local styles were showcased and important elements of the past retained. But it was done with a modern sensibility, which in some cases meant turning to earlier influences that had been abandoned. In early Creole cottages, for example, sparsely furnished rooms had multiple uses, and furniture was easily portable. With the arrival of guests (and the addition of a few armchairs) a bedroom might morph into a sitting room; a parlor might become a dining room with the addition of a table leaf or the simple rearrangement of furniture—a thoroughly modern way to live.

Even in the most pared down or modern spaces, there are, of course, some constants, the happiest of which is the architecture. New Orleans is famous for the high ceilings, fabulous French doors, and shuttered windows that were all designed to combat the heat and which exist in even the most modest of houses. Those fundamental elements are still admired and embraced, while others—massive moldings, say, or ornate fireplaces—might get a facelift. On these pages, you will see a grand, potentially heavy room that has been considerably lightened up by painting the elaborate plaster cornices, ceiling medallions, and arches the same warm white as the walls and the woodwork, bleaching the formerly dark floors, and leaving the windows curtainless. Glass-top tables, an armless sofa, and leggy armchairs seem to float through rather than anchor the room.

Elsewhere, modern mirrors or a nineteenth-century portrait that has been relieved of its crusty gilt frame hang above period mantels; a dried palmetto leaf might serve as a fire screen. These are the juxtapositions and reinventions that inject new life into old rooms. Aunt Jane's furniture is still around, but her dining chairs are now covered in graphic prints, and a Lucite coffee table might be placed in front of her ornate settee. Reinvented elements of the past might include: "old" plaster achieved with new paint effects, wrought iron crafted into a headboard or modern chandelier, once crucial mosquito netting now serving an entirely decorative purpose. And while I still know people who keep their own or their granny's queen's dress prominently displayed on an actual dress form in an actual glass case, references to Mardi Gras also are increasingly made with a more of a wink or a glance. In my friend the designer Thomas Jayne's apartment, a mask rakishly adorns the corner of a picture frame and a bowl of hand-strung vintage beads is on a table. Beads are also referenced in the brightly colored modern copies of Empire chandeliers, while ballgowns are more fetchingly recalled by the billowing unlined taffeta curtains hanging from simple rods that are a welcome antidote to pelmeted or heavily swagged window treatments.

New Orleans has long been a draw for artists, beginning with Audubon and Degas (who painted his great *Cotton Exchange in New Orleans* here in 1873), but in the last several years the city's art scene has exploded. David Halliday, Richard Sexton, and Josephine Saccabo are just three of the internationally acclaimed photographers living and working in the city. Acclaimed local painters George Dunbar, George Dureau, Raine Bedsole, and Jacqueline Bishop are represented by galleries here, as are such wider art world stars John Alexander, Hunt Slonem, and David Bates, who did a series of arresting Katrina portraits just after the storm (one of which is included here). The enthusiasm with which designers and collectors have embraced local contemporary artists and photographers, in particular, has also infused new energy into the city's interiors. As with the furniture, many of the new works are mixed with inherited pieces. In one room on these pages, a David Halliday still life leans against a trumeau mirror hanging above an antique chest. In another, a trumeau shares wall space with an enormous abstract oil.

But the galleries are by no means the only purveyors of fresh material. Once, to shop for antiques in New Orleans meant visiting a straight line of august dealers on Royal Street in the French Quarter, and there are still great treasures to be found there. But post-Katrina especially, Magazine Street has eclipsed the Quarter as a shopping mecca and has a far more eclectic mix. It is host to antiques stores that focus at least as much on Italian and Swedish furniture as French, rug dealers who sell both modern carpets and antique Orientals, contemporary home stores ranging from such brand names as Shabby Chic and Design Within Reach to locally owned shops whose keepers have gathered the best of the new with an original eye.

Lyle Saxon, who lived in New Orleans in perhaps its most stagnant era, might or might not be heartened to see a city on the move again, a city whose style is once again evolving. But he would certainly be pleased to see that in the best of the new New Orleans interiors, great care has been taken to preserve those things most cherished in the old. And he might even be forced to appreciate the mix that characterizes even the most modern of the spaces on these pages. After all, it is the careful juxtaposition of ingredients and the artful way in which they are mixed that make his beloved New Orleans cocktails so enduring. Never mind that these days an inventive young bartender might make a Sazerac by substituting cognac for the rye and orange bitters for the Peychaud's, or throw a few drops of something new into a classic Ramos Gin Fizz. They are both still every bit as delicious.

To understand the New Orleans interior design style of today, we first have to understand the city's past. Our rooms reflect a complex story spanning three centuries from colonial beginnings to antebellum grandeur to the bohemian decadence of the mid-1900s to the thriving and diverse New Orleans of the twenty-first century. Throughout this timeline, the style was driven by the convergence of French, Spanish, and African traditions in a semi-tropical climate in a unique location, a port that connects North America to the rest of the world. This convergence gave birth to jazz, Creole cuisine, wondrous architecture, and our distinct style. As antiques dealer Patrick Dunne says, "It is a style that cannot fit into the broader decorative categories that exist elsewhere."

It all started with the French colonists who brought with them their fashion and culture. Those who could afford it filled their homes with imported finery. While the colonists clung to their continental ways and wanted very much to be identified as sophisticated French rather than crass Americans, they also had to adapt quickly to the sultry climate and interact with many other cultures. The children of French colonists born in La Nouvelle Orléans were called Creoles. The same term applied to the culture and style that developed during this time. The word has come to have several different connotations today, but this definition applies here.

Peter Patout is a leading expert in Louisiana furniture, portraits, and decorative arts. When asked about the essence of New Orleans style, Patout emphasizes the Creole elements: the furniture of local masters, Louisiana portraits, and Campeche chairs. Added to this mix are the staple imports of the fine colonial house, like Paris porcelain, English ceramics, glass, silver, and decorative arts. When these elements are combined with American federal and French empire pieces and set in the south Louisiana tropics in buildings of the region's specific colonial/Caribbean design, something unmistakably specific to New Orleans emerges.

1. *The Creole Legacy*

"At its best, New Orleans style means old Southern architecture with high ceilings and windows, gorgeous plasterwork, a client who favors French antiques and an irreverent designer who can't help injecting some modern dash." —Mimi Read

LEFT
One of the characteristic elements of New Orleans style is Catholic iconography. An ornate crucifix and open-armed Madonna set a sacred tone in this Uptown dining room.

OPPOSITE
Christ is the central figure in this Uptown room among several generations of French antiques.

Saints, Altars, and Carnival Masks

Architectural and cultural traditions from the city's earliest days continue in the twenty-first century. Common in today's interiors, no matter how grand or humble, are elements of Catholic iconography, including images of saints, altars, crosses, and other religious references. Not all spiritual influence leads the flock toward the sacred, however Carnival season begins on Twelfth Night, (January 6), and takes over the city for several weeks, culminating on Mardi Gras, the last day of feasting before Lent. The Carnival season is celebrated with pageantry, parades, and society balls. Symbols of these revels—beads, crowns, and costumes—are displayed in houses from St. Charles Avenue to the Lakefront to the Lower Ninth Ward.

Voodoo was born in the late eighteenth century in the French colonies, chiefly St. Dominique (now Haiti) and New Orleans from a mixture of Roman Catholic ritual and African beliefs. Objects associated with voodoo—particularly dolls, amulets, and charms—are part of the fabric of New Orleans décor.

ABOVE

A Mardi Gras mask, antique beads, and a King Cake baby are on display in a French Quarter townhouse.

RIGHT

A Mardi Gras mask in the mix in an Uptown bedroom.

OPPOSITE

In this French Quarter parlor, a religious statue of a saint is combined with African masks.

ABOVE
There are echoes of the past in white slipcovers and fine antiques.

RIGHT
A covered porch surrounds this courtyard, creating a seamless transition between indoors and out.

OPPOSITE
The dreamy look of draping mosquito nets still has appeal.

Architecture of Centuries Past

In New Orleans, architectural elements have been adapted to the climate, creating spaces with high ceilings, transoms, huge windows, balconies, and courtyards that allow the air to circulate and blur the boundary between inside and outside. Other items born of necessity like mosquito nets, slipcovers, and grass rugs are still in use, though sometimes with a twist, throughout contemporary New Orleans interiors.

Cotton slipcovers and grass rugs have been fashionable since Colonial days when traditional "summer dress" protected Oriental rugs and velvet upholstery from mud and bugs coming in the open windows.

In old Creole days, wood floors would never have been seen. Bare wood would be covered with carpets, Canton matting, painted canvas rugs, or Oriental rugs. As in many other historic areas, painted faux finishes were used to transform what was considered unsightly raw material to simulate something fancier, a tradition that continues today.

ABOVE AND RIGHT
The foyer in this Garden District house is painted faux marble, while the living room floor has been exposed and bleached.

OPPOSITE
This Creole cottage in the French Quarter has the tall French doors typical of colonial-era rooms.

LEFT

Strong colors and contrasting lines bring intimacy to the vast spaces in this Garden District house.

OPPOSITE

Using elements of varying heights helps to balance the décor in this grand room. Draperies reach from the crown molding to the floor, accenting the height of the space while a large painting and oversized mirror match its scale. The chandelier and furnishings work to break up the visual space into an inviting interior.

OVERLEAF

This 1840 former slave quarters in the French Quarter is now an elegant pied à terre deigned by Thomas Landry. In the sitting room, a velvet daybed faces a Napoleon III commode. A pair of antique bois doré lamps sit on marble-topped iron consoles.

Scale

The economic history of New Orleans can be read by walking down the street. Mansions stand shoulder to shoulder with cottages, extravagant near humble, grand next door to petite.

In the early nineteenth-century American sector and Uptown neighborhoods, the Greek-revival giants typically dominated a large block, along with their support buildings, carriage houses, slave quarters, and garçonnières—the separate quarters provided for the young man of a wealthy household in the days when it just wouldn't do for him to stay in the same house as eligible ladies. Later in history, large estates were carved up and more modest dwellings filled in the spaces, often leaving a mansion next to a tract house next to a slave quarters in many parts of town. Even small homes and servant cottages were built with high ceilings and tall windows to suit the tropical climate.

The 350-square-foot garçonnière is packed with character and favorites from owner Peter Clepper's vast art collection. A Margaret Evangeline work from the Luminista series, a steel sheet pierced with a shotgun blast, hangs above the daybed. A Jeff Koons Balloon Dog sits on an antique table. Under the table is a bowl of Zulu coconuts, a traditional Mardi Gras talisman.

ABOVE AND OVERLEAF

This cottage a few steps from the river was built with one-by-twelve-inch wooden planks of demolished cargo barges. The bedroom opens onto the living room through a large window frame. In the dining room a chandelier made of iridescent abalone shells is juxtaposed with an antique French pine table and an eighteenth-century Gustavian sideboard.

River Legacies

Some of the materials used in nineteenth-century buildings came right off the riverboats. Ballast stone courtyards of the French Quarter and bargeboard cottages of the Irish Channel are among the legacies of the Mississippi River, along with the massive brick buildings of the Warehouse District that once held vast stores of coffee, sugar, and cotton. The old Warehouse District is now a chic neighborhood with lofts, condominiums, and art galleries.

RIGHT AND OVERLEAF

Exposed brick walls are typical of the Warehouse District. This condominium combines traditional silks and leather with contemporary acrylic and metal. A statue of Georgian Saint Nino and a prayer rug reflect the city's spiritual traditions.

"Collections are common in New Orleans houses—saints, books, candlesticks, floor-to-ceiling pictures. Catholicism is the decoration motif, with a little voodoo for good measure. Everyone has a garden and everyone exchanges plants, which turns our backyards into tropical jungles. Then there are the Mardi Gras beads and carnival memorabilia and costumes. It's all part of living in New Orleans. To me the New Orleans style is a hodgepodge of all these things. We make our eccentricity aesthetic. It is the Tennessee Williams School of Design. It is to be found nowhere else in America because no other city in America is like New Orleans."

—Lloyd Sensat, historian, preservationist, artist

II. *Eclectic to Eccentric*

As gateway to the Americas, New Orleans enjoyed a level of luxury and European imports that most of the world could only dream of. Finery of all kinds—furniture, fabrics, wines, liquors, spices, and other extravagances poured into the city along with the attendant influx of artisans, immigrants, prostitutes, criminals, and fortune-seekers. Being a port city required adopting a laissez-faire attitude. Nineteenth-century New Orleans embraced a wide range of languages, cultures, races, and economic levels. "Live and let live" was a necessity.

Only four years after the colony was founded in 1718, most of the settlement was wiped out by a hurricane. Two major fires in 1788 and 1794 destroyed most of the city's buildings. Between 1817 and 1905, more than forty-one thousand people in New Orleans died of Yellow Fever. The fact that early New Orleanians saw their colony wiped out, destroyed and decimated certainly instilled in them a sense of memento mori, which, in turn, may have been the start of some justified carpe diem.

New Orleans style today with its range from hot vivid color to cool ranges of white is a metaphor for its still diverse population and miraculous array of personalities. The style vibrates with individual expression and a large dose of whimsy.

Bywater Shotgun

Dannal Perry

"The New Orleans style of decoration is layered like our history, encompassing everything from traditional paintings to last year's Mardi Gras costumes. There is a freedom to show your own personality in your house."

—Dannal Perry

In Perry's cottage, many layers of color and hundreds of interesting objects welcome visitors. Vintage Hollywood is much in evidence in the front parlor.

ABOVE AND RIGHT

Perry placed her grandmother's pair of 1950s teal faux-leather chairs in the master bedroom. Contemporary photographs by William Greiner contrast with the collection of vintage images on the mantel and on the wall by the bed.

OPPOSITE

The space Perry calls the "Room of Popular Culture" was originally a detached kitchen and still has the large cooking hearth. Floor-to-ceiling shelves contain whimsical twentieth-century collections, including Star Wars figurines and vintage board games. A teacup chandelier completes the ensemble.

OVERLEAF

A collection of antique glass bottles Perry unearthed in the courtyard is displayed in her office.

Garden District Carriage House

Allain Bush

LEFT

In this corner, objects span four hundred years, from a seventeenth-century Spanish table and eighteenth-century trumeau mirror to a contemporary photograph by David Halliday, a mid-century modern lamp, and a 1970s disco ball.

OPPOSITE

In the parlor a French wicker chaise longue is placed in front of an eighteenth-century Italian screen and a fan of palm fronds.

"New Orleans style, like the city, has character. It is never bland or boring. There is more depth to our interiors, more than a style that just looks beautiful. There is always something added that is humorous, something that is imperfect with aged beauty, something that is unexpected."

—Allain Bush

Bargeboard Cottage

Tanga Winstead

OPPOSITE

Winstead's living room occupies a space created in the 1930s to accommodate a corner store. Among the eclectic objects are a chandelier made of wooden balls and iron and a copper tray from Iran, which serves as a fire screen. A "Katrina pole" by Simone of New Orleans leans against the wall. The clown poster by Leon Julen is a 1930 French advertisement for suspenders.

ABOVE

As a nod to New Orleans's status as the world's top coffee importer, Winstead created a coffee table by framing a burlap coffee sack and attaching baluster legs.

"In New Orleans more than anywhere else, houses reflect the personalities of the people who live in them. Our houses, like our people, are characters. We feel a need to express individuality. New Orleans style is inviting like its people. It represents a mélange of color, texture, local art, music, and decorative objects unique to the area. Here people have collections. From the bohemian approach to the well-decorated interior you see family pieces, found objects, and mementos. We mix old and new. We are not afraid to combine priceless antiques with inexpensive objects. We make art out of Mardi Gras ball invitations and parts of costumes.

We have a love of sentimental items, and we use them instead of putting them on a shelf to collect dust or only bringing them out for special occasions. New Orleans style takes the best of history and mixes it with modern touches like a pure white scheme with unexpected bursts of color."

—Tanga Winstead

OPPOSITE

The original beaded board ceiling, exposed during post-Katrina renovations, is visible throughout the house. Winstead left the century-old paint color she calls "absinthe" and covered it with a clear sealant. *Majestic Palms*, a triptych by New Orleans artists Madeline and Robert Longstreet, dominates the bedroom.

RIGHT

A platter by New York decoupage artist John Derian sits on a French butcher's block table in the dining room.

LEFT

The loft ladder ascends from the living room. Under it, a banquette from a French restaurant runs along the wall where Richard Thomas's *Queens of Carnival* and *Satchmo Festival* prints hang.

OPPOSITE

This nook off the living room is a quiet space for reading or work.

III. *Fresh Creole*

In New Orleans, home fashions are echoes of the Creole past and hints of Paris, Versailles, and Port au Prince. But a new generation of designers is reinterpreting the city's historic themes. A new chapter is being written in the epic story of New Orleans style using the old traditions in fresh, updated ways.

Fresh Creole is a term that describes interiors with an overall soft, romantic, Old New Orleans look that has been updated with new fabrics, less clutter, and artistic contemporary accents. New trends in New Orleans interiors include light, airy window treatments or none at all. Light floors and light-colored rugs are brightening New Orleans' rooms, whether it's natural grass or pale Oushak rugs, bleached wood or bright painted floors.

For centuries in New Orleans houses, kitchens were separated from main house because of the heat and the risk of fire. And kitchens were places for servants not guests. Locals' love of food and entertaining is legendary, and today's renovations often place the kitchen at the center of the living space, departing from the old tradition.

ABOVE

In Terry Gay's parlor, antiques, modern pieces, and contemporary art are combined in a setting of light, creamy tones. The romance of New Orleans is certainly present, and the historic connection is unmistakable, but the atmosphere is lighter.

OPPOSITE AND OVERLEAF

In this Uptown house, Tom Delacambre has updated colonial-style interiors with a monochrome palette with white trim and accessories.

LEFT

With its period furnishings and original paint colors, the 1799 East Indian style Pitot House is one of the purest examples of nineteenth-century Creole style. The Louisiana Landmarks Society maintains the Pitot House as a museum.

ABOVE

This French Quarter cottage, built about 1815, is an exquisite example of old Creole style. The house was painstakingly restored by the Jumer family with help from Peter Patout who helped build a collection of period Louisiana furniture. Marc Cooper advised the family on historic accuracy.

Uptown Queen Anne

Karyl Pierce-Paxton

"*New Orleans was the gateway for importing French furniture in the eighteenth and nineteenth centuries. Georgian and other period English furniture was also imported, but those styles were more popular in north Louisiana and the rest of the South. New Orleans always had an affinity for French style. Even the vernacular furniture produced in Louisiana was based on the French. It is very French to mix heirloom furniture and contemporary elements; to take old and new pieces and make them work together. New Orleans homes don't look like a decorator came in and matched everything. Rather, one finds a rich combination of textures, a little worn edges and a splash of the unexpected, a bit of surprise. Like the best examples of French art, there is a definite aspect of New Orleans style that is elegant without being prim or prissy, reflecting a looser approach to life.*

There is always a link between pieces that please you aesthetically. Whether antique pieces or contemporary art, the things that catch my eye are not so different in color and subject matter. I mix African art, Catholic art, and contemporary sculpture. What attracts me are texture, patina and richness, things that feel like New Orleans."

—Karyl Pierce-Paxton

ABOVE

The side hall is a classic New Orleans house style.

OPPOSITE

Pierce-Paxton's house is a perfect example of Fresh Creole. The essence of New Orleans style is there—the mingling of European antiques, religious icons, local art, cultural references, and eclectic personal touches enveloped in gracious nineteenth-century architecture. The focal point of the front parlor is an eighteenth-century French mirror with engaged pilasters in the form of blackamoors. The Venetian-style chandelier, matching those in the second parlor and master bedroom, contrasts with a whimsical contemporary floor lamp by Paul Gruer.

OPPOSITE

The second parlor features a pair of eighteenth-century *fauteuils à la reine* with the original tapestry upholstery, a nineteenth-century tabernacle, and architectural engravings. The sheepskin rug and the coffee table by Christopher Maier add a contemporary flair.

RIGHT

An African sculpture and a figure of a saint are displayed on a French desk with neoclassical painted decoration—a quintessential New Orleans combination.

Pierce-Paxton's view that a bit of surprise is part of New Orleans style is demonstrated in the dining room, with pumpkin orange draperies in embroidered Indian silk. The painting is by New Orleans-based artist David Harouni. Opposite the painting is an eighteenth-century Italian figure of the Infant Jesus. A crushed velvet trapunto on net from India covers the side table. The chandelier and sconces in an unrestrained floral theme are by Paul Gruer.

ABOVE LEFT

For the guest room, Pierce-Paxton made headboards out of a late eighteenth-century French daybed and painted a new top for an old iron table.

ABOVE RIGHT

Pierce-Paxton completely renovated the attic to create more living space. For the floors, she used old cypress boards salvaged from a barn. The desk is an Acadian buttermilk painted table made about 1840.

OPPOSITE

In the bathroom a claw-foot tub and an eighteenth-century chest converted into a sink cabinet set a traditional tone, updated by a sleek shower and an eccentric contemporary chandelier.

French Quarter Apartment

Thomas Jayne and Rick Ellis

From the courtyard, a stairway leads up to the balcony and Jayne and Ellis's French Quarter apartment.

"The local aesthetic is as unique as the city's history and geography. New Orleans evolved from an interaction of multiple cultures at the end of a river that links half of the North American continent and the Caribbean. The confluence of French, Spanish, and African traditions served as a springboard for vast creativity. All these elements show up in the style here. As a historicist decorator, I am always looking to history for inspiration, and New Orleans has a rich past to draw from. The cultures that helped form New Orleans offer such a wealth of beautiful influences.

Katrina emphasized how precious and fragile the historic elements of the city are. After eighty percent of the city flooded, what is being rebuilt and how it is being rebuilt holds a fascinating reflection of our time. I believe the current generation will rebuild with a reverence for history and passion for the city's future."

—Thomas Jayne

Jayne and Ellis kept most of the original floor plan intact and replicated interior elements to evoke the 1830s. In the living room, hand-painted de Gornay wallpaper surrounds the room with imagery of life in Old Louisiana. *The Story of the Mississippi*, written by Marshall McClintock and illustrated C. H. Dewitt, was the inspiration for the mural.

Antique French oil lamps and a clock decorate the living room mantle. Mario Villa candlesticks add a contemporary element on the table.

RIGHT

The sitting room features a portrait of Jayne by Don Bachardy (left) and two 1890s German wood block prints depicting Carnival costumes. The antique guest bed was once used by the Duke of Windsor when he was a guest of philanthropist Jane Engelhart at her New Jersey house Cragwood. Jayne believes the statue of Fortitude on the side table is particularly appropriate for New Orleans.

Prytania Street House

Kevin Gillentine and Vincent Bergeal

"New Orleans is a place where the old world, the new world, the humble, the grandiose, the blue blood and the outcast have all washed up together to create a quirky yet sophisticated way of living. Our tastes and aesthetics have been influenced by multiple cultures. And our climate has given us an architecture and a lifestyle of easy, flowing gracefulness, complete with high ceilings, ample porches, and large beautiful windows. Holding onto the old while embracing what's new is, in fact, nothing new to New Orleans.

I have always collected slowly. When I do buy, I buy things I know I'll love forever. Because of this, I have been able to put together a home that is not only beautiful, but also meaningful. Each piece has a story, a memory. I believe that putting together a beautiful room is actually quite easy. But when you create a space that is both beautiful and interesting, then you have something special."

—Kevin Gillentine

ABOVE

The mix of European furniture in the entry hall includes a painted Directoire armchair, an Italian commode, and a large urn by Cartel. The newel post is original to the house and is made from mahogany with birds eye maple accents.

OPPOSITE

The seductive living room of this grand 1885 mansion features a French Directoire daybed, a 1940s onyx top coffee table, Directoire side chairs, and a pair of French bergeres gathered around a zebra skin rug.

Gillentine created a warm ochre color for the dining room inspired by natural history book plates from the same period as the house. The Louis XVI chairs are upholstered in a Brunschwig and Fils fabric with an organic design that echoes a collection of framed botanical prints by German photographer Karl Blossfeldt.

ABOVE LEFT

The informal family room combines traditional and contemporary with a pair of Barcelona chairs, a Swedish commode, and a Tibetan painted table.

ABOVE RIGHT AND OPPOSITE

In the kitchen a French bistro table, Tibetan painted cabinet, and 1920s portrait by Pepe of Barcelona are juxtaposed with metal mesh dining chairs. A French farm table serves as the kitchen island with vintage bins from an old French thread factory used as storage below.

Lakeview Cottage

Karina Gentinetta

RIGHT
Grays and balcks create a grisaille effect, puctuated by the gilding on the lamps and mirror and the crimson seat.

OPPOSITE AND OVERLEAF
The living room has painted wood floors, a threadbare oriental rug, and rescued treasures like the antique barrel chairs and French day bed Gentinetta painted and reupholstered.

"In just one stormy night, Hurricane Katrina took everything—my home, my life-long possessions, my security—everything, except my creativity and my ambition to not be defeated. As I began to rebuild my world with limited resources and amidst a devastating reality of sheer destruction, I began to discover the beauty and glamour of vintage finds. My surroundings became a melange of beautiful things that time had forgotten and tossed away."

—Karina Gentinetta

OPPOSITE

Among the gray and white tones, Belgian linen, and peach Fortuny silk, are a few items that survived Katrina. The mirror, an inexpensive piece with a plastic frame, emerged from the mud with a beautifully corroded antique look that Gentinetta calls "Katrina Patina."

RIGHT

Leather chairs and an old wood table add a rustic element to the kitchen.

In the entry, antique and twentieth-century pieces mix.

Light curtains, a grass rug, and French and Italian furniture create a romantic look in the master bedroom.

French Quarter Apartment

Peter Patout

RIGHT

The furnishings are contemporary with the nineteenth-century building; the trompe l'oeil grisaille paper screens were made in Paris in the 1810s, and the Louisiana portrait of a Creole lady holding a rose is dated 1838. Light pours in through tall New Orleans windows unencumbered by draperies.

OVERLEAF

The kitchen is open to living room, a contemporary plan that would not have existed in the old Creole days.

"Technically the colonial era ended in 1803 with the Louisiana Purchase, but culturally we continued to be French with provincial tastes and ways. I try to convey the feeling of another century in my design."

—Peter Patout

OPPOSITE

Pheasant feathers and palm fronds make a unique firescreen. The coffee service on the Empire center table is Vieux Paris porcelain.

RIGHT

The rich color of the original living room floor is echoed in the new bannister. Engravings of classical urns line the stairwell.

The large center hall is typical of late-nineteenth-century Victorian houses. A painted and mirrored armoire faces a white-slipcovered canapé. Bright pink velvet pillows pick up colors in the *Chocolates* triptych while the watery blue of the sea glass chandelier reflects color of the armoire.

Victorian Center Hall Mansion

Charles and Jacquelyn Stern with Tanga Winstead

"I like furniture to have a history and to show imperfections. We have a wood table and an iron daybed that were used during the Civil War and constructed to be taken apart and carried until the soldiers got to the next place to set up camp. I choose things that I love, not things that match, and I like to combine old and new, so the rooms have no preconceived design scheme. It's a blend of funky and sophisticated just like the city."

—Jacquelyn Stern

In the Sterns' music room, a shabby slipcovered chaise in light pink floral softens the formality of the secretary in chalk green with an antique pavilion striped chair.

Crisp white slipcovers, white-framed mirrors, and a white-painted armoire create a fresh look in the family room. Vintage pieces include the chandelier and the pendants over the dining table, which were originally part of the chandelier. Stained glass in the bay window is original to the house.

The kitchen features a moveable island created from an antique storage piece with drawers. Casters were added along with a high gloss painted blue top. Food is stored in ball and mason jars on shelves above the copper farmers sink, which is surrounded with a blue toile skirt. Childhood memorabilia like the tricycle is featured on top of the hutch in a typical New Orleans contrast to the heirloom china and crystal inside. Painted chairs surround the farm table for a rustic European look. The antique green ladder with rope extensions is actually used on a regular basis.

In the entry, a hot-pink sofa is set against dark brown walls. Marshall painted the wood floors in a faux-marble design. The bold colors and abstract paintings by New Orleans artist Katie Rafferty give a modern feel to this otherwise antique setting.

Garden District Mansion

Ned Marshall

"Powerful color is about balance. It's like having a living room done in silk and satin. It's much more chic if you add some straw or something rough. With color, it's the same principle. You tame strong color by adding a lot of neutrals to the room—woods, browns, beiges, creams, golds, silvers. And you do not make every room in the house wildly colored, which would feel like a riot. I try to achieve a certain rhythm of color so that nothing is jarring but nothing is beiged to death either."

—Ned Marshall

ABOVE

A grass rug and subtle faux finish set the stage for a classical, but soft, parlor.

RIGHT

Fluted columns separate the entrance hall and parlor.

OPPOSITE

In the stair landing/entrance hall, Marshall painted the fourteen-foot high walls in silver stripes using radiator paint. The décor is a mix of antique, neoclassical, and new pieces includes transitional Louis XV style chairs, a midcentury glass and chrome table, a plaster cast of an ancient Roman foot, and a rusting, architectural finial.

Marshall created the living room wall color, which he calls "Hermes Box Orange," by mixing several different orange paints. The vivid tone makes what would otherwise be a massive cold space warm and vibrant.

OVERLEAF AND SECOND OVERLEAF Marshall painted the dining room walls the same dark chocolate brown as the entry to bring intimacy to the space. The rich color is a dramatic background for the blue and white fabrics.

Audubon Park House

Gerrie Bremermann

OPPOSITE
In the front parlor, light neutral colors create a calming atmosphere. With contemporary fabrics and delicate forms, the furniture avoids any suggestion of stuffiness or heaviness. The chairs and canapé are nineteenth-century French.

ABOVE
The neutral palette continues in the living room where a large painting by Hall Larson of Santa Fe provides a punch of color and a contemporary flare. The bronze statue is by David Pearson, also of Santa Fe.

"The atmosphere here makes New Orleans style different from any other in the world, not only the tropical temperature but also the luxurious life around us. Our vibrant array of architecture, art, food, and music influences the way we decorate and creates a spirit that makes this city what it is. We have a unique conglomeration of talent. The artistic spirit is what makes New Orleans special and helped the city survive Katrina and countless disasters before.

Other places borrow elements of New Orleans style, but it doesn't work the same way in other climates. Other places don't have the same kind of inspiration for creativity we see here every day. The tropical temperature inspires a light, neutral color palette, and simple, airy window treatments. This combines with traditions of French and Victorian furnishings, plus elements of local architecture like wrought iron. New Orleans style today is airy, eclectic, classic-with-contemporary, filled with Catholic iconography and family pieces."

—Gerrie Bremermann

OPPOSITE

Dancing Graces, a triptych by New Orleans artist George Dureau, hangs above a nineteenth-century English sideboard.

RIGHT

An antique trumeau mirror is the focal point of the second-floor study. It is complemented by other local finds, including an eighteenth-century French armchair, a Louis XVI bookcase, an eighteenth-century walnut desk, and an Oushak carpet.

OVERLEAF

Simple but luxuriant gray silk curtains allow the eighteenth-century Portuguese/Spanish bed and mirrored cross to be come the focal point of the master bedroom.

Uptown Restoration

Jaye Parish and Ed Graf

"For us, finding a hundred-year-old storm damaged house after Katrina and restoring it was a way of rebuilding our lives, the city, our home—a way of recovering and being part of the city's recovery. New Orleanians are hopeless romantics, with a love for things tarnished and discarded, found yet reinvented. A product of the city's past, New Orleans style is an assemblage of bits and pieces of the city's diverse culture, its exotic heritage, the distinctive character of architectural relics merged with peeling paint, decaying grandeur, the music, the art, the food and, of course, the climate. Perhaps the one thing that distinguishes New Orleans style most from other places is its soul and its patina.

The city is timeless, yet always evolving and reinventing itself. The design attitude now is much more vibrant, and perhaps more experimental, more open to modern improvements as long as they do not compromise the allure. It's an attitude infused with a new energy, a new spirit, but it still holds tightly to those distinctive characteristics which make the city unique. We embrace our culture more now than ever before, because we've had to defend it to the rest of the world."

—Jaye Parish

The library was furnished as two seating areas. In one, Parish mixed a nineteenth-century Louis XV-style sofa, vintage Florentine tables, antique French folding chair, and modern brass lamps. On the other side Philippe Starck "Ghost Chairs" surround a cypress table made from salvaged wood drugstore columns. Antique Italian giltwood chandeliers hang above both areas. A Louis Philippe mirror hangs over the shuttered window.

OPPOSITE

The master bath is a magical blend of colors and textures. Parish created the wall finish and silver leafed an antique tub herself. The couple found the Azulejos tiles for the shower while vacationing in Lisbon.

RIGHT

The second floor hall contains an intriguing mix of old and new. The back of an antique French saint's niche shows the original plaster and lathe work with antique mirror inserted. On the other side is a recessed sink area in the master bath. The very contemporary hanging sculpture, entitled *Membrane*, is by Jonathan Bouknight. A red Fungo stool adds a splash of color.

RIGHT

In the study, a Bertoia chair and hand-painted cabinet sit in front of one of Parish's own paintings.

OPPOSITE

Parish's studio is an enclosed porch with painted wood floors and French embroidered linen curtains. A Lucite luggage rack serves as a table with a modern steel chair.

OVERLEAF

White is the dominant color with black, red and blue accents. Herman Leonard photographs of Billy Holiday and Dexter Gordon from the 1940s enliven the room while a Harry Bertoia "diamond chair" makes a statement in red. A Valerie Bunnell ceramic sculpture stands by the antique cast-iron fire screen. Small sculptures on the mantel are by Andrew Bascal and Joy Gauss.

ABOVE

Another Bertoia chair, this time the "bird" in white with an ottoman.

RIGHT

The coffee tables are by Florence Knoll. Parish painted the fabric and wood of two midcentury chairs. A nineteenth-century Italian mirror is next to a vintage Louisiana cabinet.

OPPOSITE

The sleek kitchen island incorporates an antique French frieze. An Italian hood floats above. A ceiling fan adds more contemporary flair.

RIGHT

A ceramic wall sculpture by Michaelene Walsh hangs over the windowseat opposite the kitchen island.

The grandeur of the Greek Revival architecture in New Orleans encourages formal and elegant interior design solutions. The fresh, relaxed kind of elegance in today's rooms respects the classic proportions and architectural shell. Three centuries of furniture are updated with contemporary fabrics, art, and accessories.

The way living space evolved to reflect the character of New Orleanians in the nineteenth century continues today in a less formal atmosphere, during a time of individual expression. New New Orleans style is one step closer contemporary than Fresh Creole, sometimes a half and half blend of old and new pieces, sometimes very updated surroundings, sometimes very new but with an air of New Orleans old romance. These interiors feature several generations of inherited pieces updated with modern fabrics, combined with new pieces and local, contemporary art. Some houses stand out as showcases for the city's multitude of talented sculptors and painters. These interiors are designed around the art and for the art. The architecture becomes part of the tableau.

IV. *New New Orleans Style*

"New Orleans has resisted the homogeneity taking place in other parts of the country. There is an appreciation and celebration here of the unique, the genuine, the different. Even though we are steeped in history, we have a tradition of creating something new from the clashing of cultures. New from old—that's us, and that's our future."

— Ann Koerner, owner of Ann Koerner Antiques

In the double-parlor of this 1856 mansion, classic French chairs combine with modern pieces and a 1960s footed table by San Francisco designer John Dickenson. The original column screen dividing the two spaces has been removed, making the dramatic triple arch between them a dominant sculptural element.

Coliseum Square Mansion

John Chrestia

"New Orleans style does not resemble the cliché that people think of—images of red velvet and crystal chandeliers. It is an evolution of sophisticated periods and lifestyles on a continuum between the past and the future."

—John Chrestia

LEFT

Original leaded-glass pocket doors separate the living room and dining room. Chrestia found the French-designed plaster of paris chandelier at a New York gallery.

BELOW

A painting by Jim Richard hangs above a settee from the studio of Emile-Jacques Ruhlmann.

OPPOSITE

A bold abstract painting by Ed Whiteman hangs over the nineteenth-century marble mantel with a Margaret Evangeline wall sculpture to the left.

LEFT

The kitchen features a copper-top table and a seating area with contemporary lighting and art by Deborah Pelias.

ABOVE

A painting by Pat Trivigno adds drama to the master bedroom. The chest of drawers is by Paul McCobb.

In this grand nineteenth-century house, Villarreal preserved the original detailing—denticulated cornices and plaster ceiling ornament—and introduced a blue and gold color scheme, which is punctuated with bold contemporary art. Custom-designed high-backed seat furniture breaks down the scale of the rooms.

Jose and Ileana Suquet Residence

Rodney Santana Villarreal

"*This eclectic blend of modern and old is where I see the future of New Orleans interior design heading, not minimalist, but clean in a way that allows you to appreciate the architecture and the textures that make old buildings so wonderful.*"

—Rodney Santana Villarreal

OPPOSITE

A silkscreen by New York-based Brazilian artist Laura Calhoun hangs in the dining room. The glass sculpture is by Dino Rosin.

RIGHT

In the family room, a branch lamp refinished in silver leaf complements a screen of antique mirror glass and Venetian silver leaf.

LEFT

In the guestroom, Villarreal placed high valences and a matching canopy of Bergamo "Oyster" silk to raise the eye.

OPPOSITE

Six Dalí prints decorate a dining area in the kitchen along with a Palazzo chandelier.

Uptown House

Bryan Batt and Tom Cianfichi

THIS SPREAD AND OVERLEAF
Batt and Cianfichi's Caribbean-style home features a sunny living room they call "the tree house" with painted wood floors and an artistic mixture of antiques and modern pieces. Above the mantel is *Prince Charming Kissing Snow White* by New Orleans artist Blake Boyd, executed in metallic leaf on clay. Batt found the laughing terra-cotta bust while traveling. Three landscapes over the iron console are by Susan Downing.

"Like the perfect impromptu cocktail party, great New Orleans style is never fussy or forced rather it's an effortless colorful mix. I think the old New Orleans attitude of 'Anything Goes' shows in our interiors and is even stronger since Katrina."

—Bryan Batt

OVERLEAF

Downstairs from the sunny living room, the den is cozy and intimate. Warm gray walls are a perfect neutral background for colorful, local art like the James Beaman painting above the mantel. A collection of midcentury glass is featured on a Mario Villa coffee table.

In the dining room, Mario Villa metal swag chairs surround a custom travertine table and are combined with antique pieces and a chandelier that belonged to Batt's mother. The large abstract painting is by Evert Witte.

The bedroom is all about textures with a goat skin chest, cowhide rugs, Mongolian lamb pillows, vintage brass lamps, modern lacquer side tables, and, for or a touch of whimsy, an antique French bulldog pull. Another James Beaman painting adds a splash of color.

Vaccari's showroom occupies the first floor of his 1853 St. Charles Avenue mansion, and his apartment spreads throughout the second and third floors. In the parlor Vaccari created a soft and romantic space with a sizzling, contemporary edge. Featured items are a French mirror and crystal chandelier, a painting on steel by Margaret Evangeline, a Maison Jansen coffee table, 1970s Italian table lamps, and sofa and chairs of his design.

St. Charles Avenue Classic

Jon Vaccari

"I really love renovation, seeing beauty in the bones of a place, and giving it a new life: keeping an Old-World charm, but creating a new flow for the way we live now."

—Jon Vaccari

In the dining room French chairs mix with 1940s Italian sconces and a 1950s French mirror. The glass table sits on twentieth-century Italian, bronze rams heads.

OVERLEAF

The white and silver palette of the parlor and dining room transitions into a more relaxed, colorful den.

In a hallway just off the foyer of the midcentury modern house, Rufty combined a Directoire canape with a modern glass table and works by Atlanta artist Steven Seinberg. Rufty often uses a high-gloss wall finish to emphasize the natural light from traditional New Orleans floor to ceiling windows.

OVERLEAF

After moving from a very traditional home after Katrina, the Rabalaises found that their new modern house was a perfect canvas to reinvent the antiques they had spent years collecting and restoring. In the living room, a painting by New Orleans artist James Beaman blends with an antique French canapé and midcentury pierced brass lamps.

Old Metairie Modern

Jennifer and Kenny Rabalais with Melissa Rufty

"I've certainly embraced the formality and grandeur of New Orleans. But I also love the underbelly, the fun and carefree wildness. You can start the night in a fabulous landmark restaurant and end up in a dive bar under a bridge. It's that same dichotomy that is so unique to New Orleans design. There are all walks of life around you, and we're all comfortable in the mix.

Southerners are great storytellers. So it's no surprise that New Orleans homes have a distinctive voice. Designers from all over the world shop here for that quirky piece with a past that can give a room its soul. The city has taught me that it's not about perfection. Fine antiques are wonderful, but lesser things can tell a great story and convey a sense of place."

—Melissa Rufty

LEFT

Rufty covered the couple's Louis XVI dining chairs in a python vinyl and repurposed them as kitchen chairs.

OPPOSITE

Artwork by Amanda Talley and slipcovered chairs create a cool and casual space in a hall.

OVERLEAF

Rufty split the Rabalaises' eighteenth-century dining table into two demilunes and combined them with a pair of antique gilt mirrors. Custom silk velvet benches in green tiger flank the front door. The white ceramic floors and laquered walls create a gleaming background.

LEFT

Rufty created an aquatic fantasy in the powder room. Heirloom Louis XVI sconces are combined with the handpainted de Gournay wallpaper.

OPPOSITE

A magnolia leaf sculpture by Bradley Sabin blooms in the hallway to the master bedroom. The contemporary art installation is combined with a Louis XVI console and mirror.

LaLaurie Mansion

Lee Ledbetter

OPPOSITE

In the neoclassical double parlor Ledbetter created dramatic black and white scenes. 1930s Swedish chairs flank a table by Donald Deskey. The painting is by Pat Steir.

RIGHT

The ornate doorway frames a large photograph by Dawn Dedeaux. The collection of photographs includes works by Merry Alpern, Carrie Mae Weems, Jack Pierson, Robert Mapplethorpe, and Sally Mann.

Uptown House

Jim Mounger with John Crestia

"What I love best about New Orleans is the food, the people, and the high ceilings. My house is 1900s on the outside and twenty-first century on the inside, which always gives visitors a surprise."

—Jim Mounger

The main living area was completely reconfigured. Four steel-pipe columns replaced supporting walls and follow the line of the original center hall. Walls and ceiling were painted all one color to create a consistent background for the art.

Furnishings sit away from the walls, leaving more hanging space for art. The space features a blown-glass chandelier by Dale Chihuly and a triple portrait of Barbra Streisand as Yentil by Deborah Kass.

OPPOSITE

The serene blue of the Chihuly chandelier is repeated in a painting by New York artist Maria Scotti.

ABOVE

In front of a puzzle piece collage by Al Souza, a white chaise is striking but not distracting.

ABOVE

Even the kitchen has clean, simple lines. Photographs of the moon by Italian artist Luca Massoni make a dramatic statement on the back wall. Two paintings by Dallas artist Linda Ridgeway flank the kitchen entry. The old New Orleans tradition of pocket doors inspired an updated version in the dining room, breakfast room, and kitchen, which can be separated into three spaces or opened up into one continuous room.

RIGHT

A mobile/chandelier by Tim Prentice revolves slowly above the dining table. A wall sculpture by Margaret Evangeline hangs above the buffet (left), with photographs by Italian Giacomo Costa on the facing and end walls.

LEFT

The master bedroom stretches across the entire front of the house. A platform-style bed floats away from the wall, leaving space for a colorful triptych by local artist Allison Stewart.

RIGHT ABOVE

Even the master bath doubles as an art gallery, featuring a painting by Robert Warrens.

RIGHT BELOW

In the guest bath, Chrestia created a counter from a steel tool box designed for a pickup truck bed.

OPPOSITE

In the gracefully curving stairwell, the architecture frames the art. *Desire of Power, Power of Desire* by Robert Colescott is on view under the turn of the stairs. *Ronald McDonald*, four panels in clay and metal leaf by Blake Boyd, hangs on the left wall.

RIGHT

The house was built by Dr. Dominique Durac and completed around 1860. It has the only Victorian octagonal facade in the French Quarter. Inside, the shape of the building creates unexpected turns and flow from one room to another.

French Quarter Victorian

Arthur Roger

"In building an art collection you strive to achieve a dynamic that results from showing works in relationship to one another. In our décor there is often a layeringive to achieve a dynamic tmixed in with the fine pieces layeringive to achieve a dynam. This historic building in the French Quarter presents an added opportunity to show the relationship of an art collection to the unique architectural lines of the house."

—Arthur Roger

In the den are a portrait of Andy Warhol by Greg Gorman and *Staff*, an aluminum sculpture by Ida Kohlmeyer.

Art by Luis Cruz Azaceta hangs between the windows in the den. The bronze head is by Stephen Paul Day.

In the dining room, a Christopher Maier table and chairs are set against a large mixed-media piece by Whitfield Lovell entitled *Still*. Richard Jolley glass on the table and a 1920s Venetian chandelier above add color and sparkle. *Black Snake* by David Bates, a landscape triptych by Elemore Morgan Jr., and a cabinet decorated with gilded wings, also by Maier, complete the room.

The second floor landing is an airy stage for Dale Chihuly's *Ruby Red Chandelier*. On the wall is *The Rain of Huizilopochtli*, a drawing by James Drake.

In the master bedroom are a self-portrait by Deborah Kass and *Swan Dance*, a glowing work by Blake Boyd in clay and gold leaf. On the small table are Franco Mondini-Ruiz "Horses" found objects.

ABOVE

The guest bedroom has a strong Hurricane Katrina theme. *After the Flood*, a Robert Polidori photograph hangs above the bed with David Bates's *The Flood* over the mantel and John Geldersma's *Spirit Pole* on the left.

OPPOSITE

Rogers's renovated attic is a very angular and contemporary media room with photographs by John Waters and Greg Gorman.

ABOVE

In the garconiere/guesthouse, the long room serves as a combined living and dining room. *Woman with Glasses* from the Katrina Portraits series by David Bates hangs on a rough plaster and brick wall.

OPPOSITE

Ida Kohlmeyer 's *Synthesis* is the centerpiece of the living space.

Broadmoor Bungalow

Curtis Herring

"We have so much to draw from creatively in New Orleans. Our deep, multicultural history, dramatic weather, a seemingly constant social calendar, and a very relaxed and open-minded populace, all make interior design projects here fun and meaningful. One thing I notice about New Orleans style and the New Orleanian in general, is individuality. No matter what the finished look is, be it contemporary, modern, eclectic, French, traditional, or something in between, my clients are willing to try something new and to be a little different from their neighbors. New Orleans style is eclectic. Most people here have inherited antique pieces that need to be incorporated into the fabric of the interior. There is also a general love of contemporary art, French and English antiques as well as clean-line contemporary furnishings and funky "found art" items from travel abroad or visits to Magazine Street. All of these things woven together create an individual, sophisticated interior."

—Curtis Herring

After Katrina, Herring filled his home with things he really loves. In the living room an Oushak carpet picks up soft ochre tones in the abstract painting by Allison Stewart. An American Empire secretary, made in New Orleans about 1820–40, survived both the Civil War and Katrina. Herring designed the end tables and coffee tables.

OPPOSITE

The dining room features a 1940s chandelier, a painting by Gaither Pope, and a table and Seignoret chairs, also Katrina survivors.

ABOVE

In the kitchen, Herring combined a tulip table with Eames molded fiberglass chairs. Above the vintage phone is a David Harouni painting.

OPPOSITE

Chinese motifs in the fabric of the shade refer to the Chinese Export porcelain platter on the counter.

RIGHT

In the entry foyer a painting by local artist Jean Geraci hangs above a Victorian table.

Esplanade Avenue Mansion

Sean Cummings with L. M. Pagano

"This house is very rich in history. 'Count' Arnaud Casenave (founder of Arnaud's Restaurant) and his famous daughter, Germaine Wells, wre among its owners. It was the home of Daniel Lanois's Kingsway Studio and later owned by Nicolas Cage. Sean and I were extraordinarily concerned with celebrating and honoring the mansion's history and, more generally, what is innately New Orleans and its jumble of influences, the religiosity, the constancy of crumbling elegance, the continuing musical legacy, the decadence, the rituals. We chose to interpret this with a modern, unexpected twist.

We incorporated old with new, included found and vintage pieces, but kept it uncluttered and elegant. We incorporated and restored architectural details but kept the pallet monochrome to emphasize the space instead of some complicated color scheme."

—L. M. Pagano

The Swarovski Cascade chandelier designed by Vincent Van Duysen was commissioned for the entrance hall of house.

LEFT

Several African elements honor the Senegalese/West African historical link and presence in New Orleans. A highly carved wooden Senegalese antique fertility bed which has been silver-chromed is on display in the living room/music room.

ABOVE AND OPPOSITE

The dining room table is eleven feet long and handmade out of two-hundred-year-old walnut in the style of a seventeenth-century Italian refectory table.

OPPOSITE

The grand entrance hall opens to the dining room where simplicity in the design highlights the graceful nineteenth-century architecture. Above the mantel is a painting by David Harouni

ABOVE

The large second-floor work and play area combines contemporary furnishings, an antique mirror and another work by David Harouni.

Uptown Updated

Holden and Dupuy

"I've been everywhere, but there's no place like New Orleans. It's not Europe, but it's not America. We don't always have money here, but we do have style."

—Ann Holden

An example of contemporary style with New Orleans flair, this dining and living room features a large artwork by Nicole Charbonnet, contemporary furniture, and a few well-placed antiques. The Greek key motif, very common in New Orleans interiors, appears as a wide band of gold leaf instead of crown molding.

OPPOSITE

In the dinning area a long glass table is surrounded by Donghia Anziano chairs.

Ann Koerner Antiques
4201 Magazine Street
New Orleans, Louisiana 70115

Antiques on Jackson
1028 Jackson Avenue
New Orleans, Louisiana 70130

Arthur Roger Gallery
432 Julia Street
New Orleans, Louisiana 70130

Balzac Antiques
3506 Magazine Street
New Orleans, Louisiana 70115

Bremermann Designs
3943 Magazine Street
New Orleans, Louisiana 70115

Bush Antiques
2109 Magazine Street
New Orleans, Louisiana 70130

**Catherine Cottrell
Interior Design**
3638 Magazine Street
New Orleans, Louisiana 70115

Cole Pratt Gallery
3800 Magazine Street
New Orleans, Louisiana 70115

Crestia Staub Pierce
7219 Perrier Street
New Orleans, Louisiana 70118

Curtis Herring Interior Design
1639 S. Jefferson Davis Parkway
New Orleans, Louisiana 70125

Dop Antiques
300 Jefferson Highway
New Orleans, Louisiana 70121

Dunn and Sonnier Antiques
2138 Magazine Street
New Orleans, Louisiana 70130

The Garden Gate
701 Jefferson Highway
Jefferson, Louisiana 70121

Glen Armand Furniture
1019 Twin Bridges Road
Alexandria, Louisiana 71303

Guthrie Contemporary Gallery
315 Magazine Street
New Orleans, Louisiana 70115

Hazelnut
5515 Magazine Street
New Orleans, Louisiana 70115

Holden & Dupuy Interior Design
839 Saint Charles Avenue
New Orleans, Louisiana 70130

Interior Designs II
3814 Magazine Street
New Orleans, Louisiana 70115

Jaye Parish, J3 Design
1807 Robert Street
New Orleans, Louisiana 70115

Jayne Design Studio
210 Fifth Avenue
New York 10001

**Jon Vaccari Design
and Antiques**
1912 Saint Charles Avenue
New Orleans, Louisiana 70130

Karla Katz Antiques
4017 Magazine Street
New Orleans, Louisiana 70115

Karina Gentinetta Disengo
3652 Magazine Street
New Orleans, Louisiana 70115

Kevin Gillentine Gallery
3917 Magazine Street
New Orleans, Louisiana 70115

Kisabeth Furniture
270 Decorative Center
Dallas, Texas 75207

Lee Ledbetter & Associates
1055 St. Charles Avenue
New Orleans, Louisiana 70130

Resources

Linens, Lace, and Lunacy
Metairie, Louisiana

Lucullus Antiques
107 North Main Street
Breaux Bridge, Louisiana 70517

Lum Vintage Lighting
3806 Magazine Street
New Orleans, Louisiana 70115

Mac Maison
3963 Magazine Street
New Orleans, Louisiana 70115

McConnell's Furniture Refinishing
10435 Gurney Road
Baker, Louisiana 70714

Ma Puce Antiques
5227 Tchoupitoulas Street
New Orleans, Louisiana 70115

Ned Marshall Interior Design/Pastiche
2601 Camp Street
New Orleans, Louisiana 70130

Marsh Garden Decor
355 Iris Avenue #D
Jefferson, Louisiana 70121

MMR Interiors
3806 Magazine Street
New Orleans, Louisiana 70115

New Orleans Auction Gallery
801 Magazine Street
New Orleans, Louisiana 70130

Peter Patout Antiques
1111 Bourbon Street
New Orleans, Louisiana 70116

Pierce-Paxton Design Studio
1000 Bourbon Street
New Orleans, Louisiana 70116

Plant Gallery: Home and Garden
2033 N Highway 190
Covington, Louisiana 70433

Plum
5430 Magazine Street
New Orleans, Louisiana 70115

Rug Chic
4240 Highway 22, Suite 6
Mandeville, Louisiana 70471

Shades of Light
1123 Josephine Street
New Orleans, Louisiana 70130

Shady Side Pottery
3823 Magazine Street
New Orleans, Louisiana 70115

Sitting Duck Gallery
4440 Earhart Boulevard A
New Orleans, Louisiana 70125

Soniat Antiques
1139 Chartres Street
New Orleans, Louisiana 70116

Specialty Carpet of New Orleans
560 Brooklyn Avenue
New Orleans, Louisiana 70121

Tanga Winstead Designs
4882 Annunciation Street
New Orleans, Louisiana 70115

Uptowner Antiques
3828 Magazine Street
New Orleans, Louisiana 70115

Villa Vici
2930 Magazine Street
New Orleans, Louisiana 70115

Rodney Santana Villarreal Interior Design
1032 Esplanade Avenue

New Orleans, Louisiana 70116

Wirthmore Antiques
3727 Magazine Street
New Orleans, Louisiana 70115

The inspiration for this book came from the talented designers, architects, and decorators who transform interiors into works of art. The depth of beauty and significance they create never ceases to amaze me. It has been a huge privilege to work with Bryan Batt and Tom Cianfichi, John Chrestia, Tom Delcambre, Karina Gentinetta, Kevin Gillentine, Curtis Herring, Ann Holden and Ann Dupuy, Lee Ledbetter, Ned Marshall, L. M. Pagano, Peter Patout, Dannal Perry, Melissa Rufty, and Jon Vaccari. And I owe a special thanks to Thomas Jayne, who introduced me to The Monacelli Press while photographing his book, The Finest Rooms in America.

Some artists, designers, and antiques experts I have worked with and admired for many years, and it is an extra joy to have their collaboration in this project, especially Allain Bush, Rodney Villarreal, Karyl Paxton, Gerrie Bremermann, and Tanga Winstead, who went above and beyond to help.

It might look like all glamour, but photographing a home can be exhausting and messy, and yet people let me take over their houses, move their stuff, and generally cause chaos. I appreciate the gracious spirit of everyone who has invited me in, especially Arthur Roger, the Stern family, Shawn and Marie Gibbs, Larry and Cherry Courville, the Howards, Sean Cummings, Tommy and Lisa Flower, and the Heebes.

It was my goal from the beginning to use comments from the people who really know and create New Orleans style. For more fantastic prose than I could have hoped for, I am grateful to the people mentioned above and others who made the additional contribution of putting their ideas into words for me, especially Mimi Reed, who is to language as Michelangelo is to marble.

I am beyond honored to have the perfect introduction by the awesome Julia Reed. Above all, I might never have done this book without her enthusiastic encouragement when I first had the idea.

Acknowledgments

I always turn to Mikko Macchione for writing help and direction. On this book, he came through again with insightful editing and a few much needed laughs. Someone has to make sure I don't take myself too seriously.

I owe great thanks to my editor, Elizabeth White, and the Monacelli Press for expert guidance in the creative process and making my vision possible.

I would not accomplish much without my mom, Cynthia, a wonderful writer and tireless helper in books and in life. I am inspired by my sweet son, Leonardo, who at age 4 made the painting on page 33, commissioned by Uncle Rodney, and I am grateful to Ector, my most significant other, for serene support and for our baby, Gabriel.

Mostly, I am grateful to everyone who loves New Orleans and makes it what it is. I am so lucky to live here.